This book belongs to:

_____

Meditative Manadalas: A Coloring Book
Illustrations by Stacy Cobb
Copyright 2019 Stacy-Sue Cobb

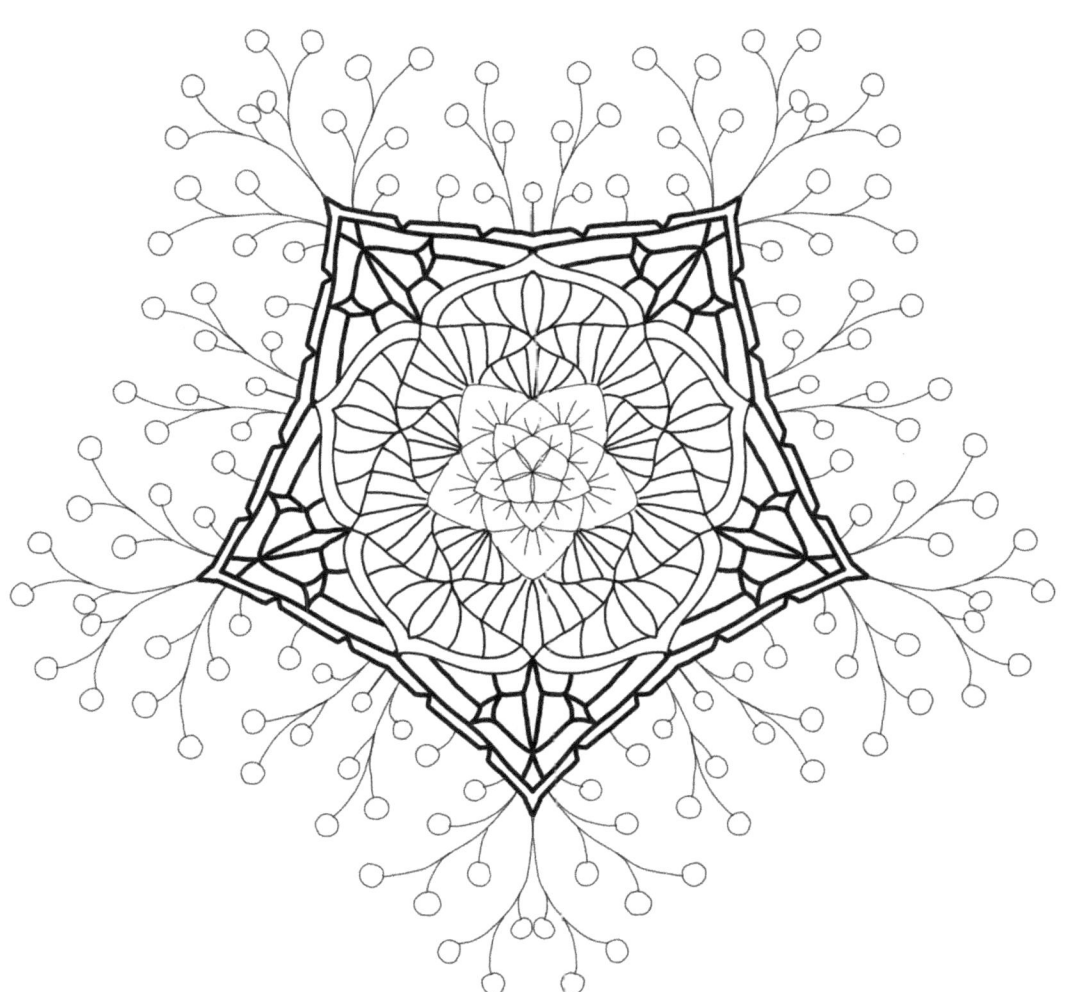

Plate 1

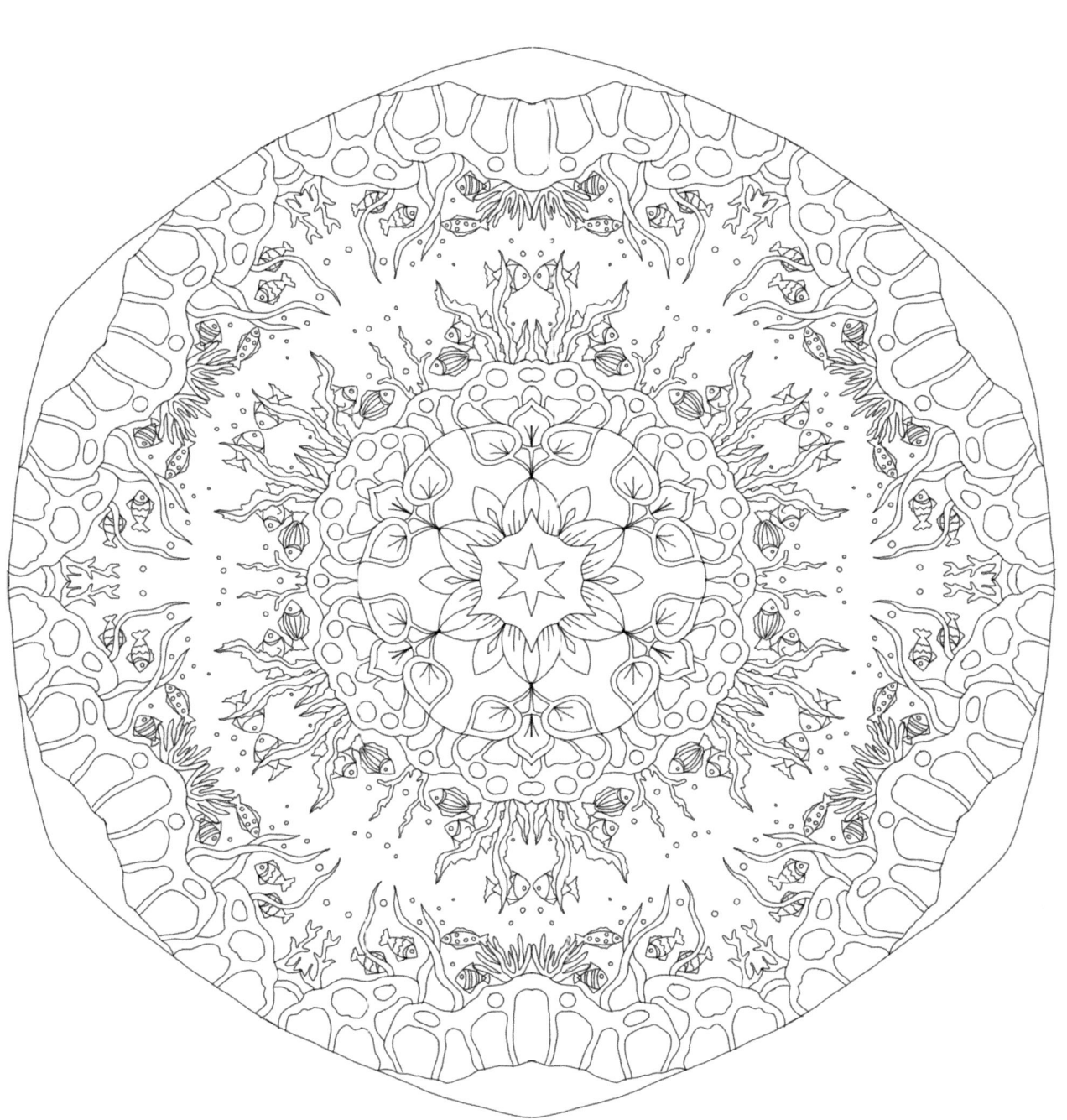

Plate 2

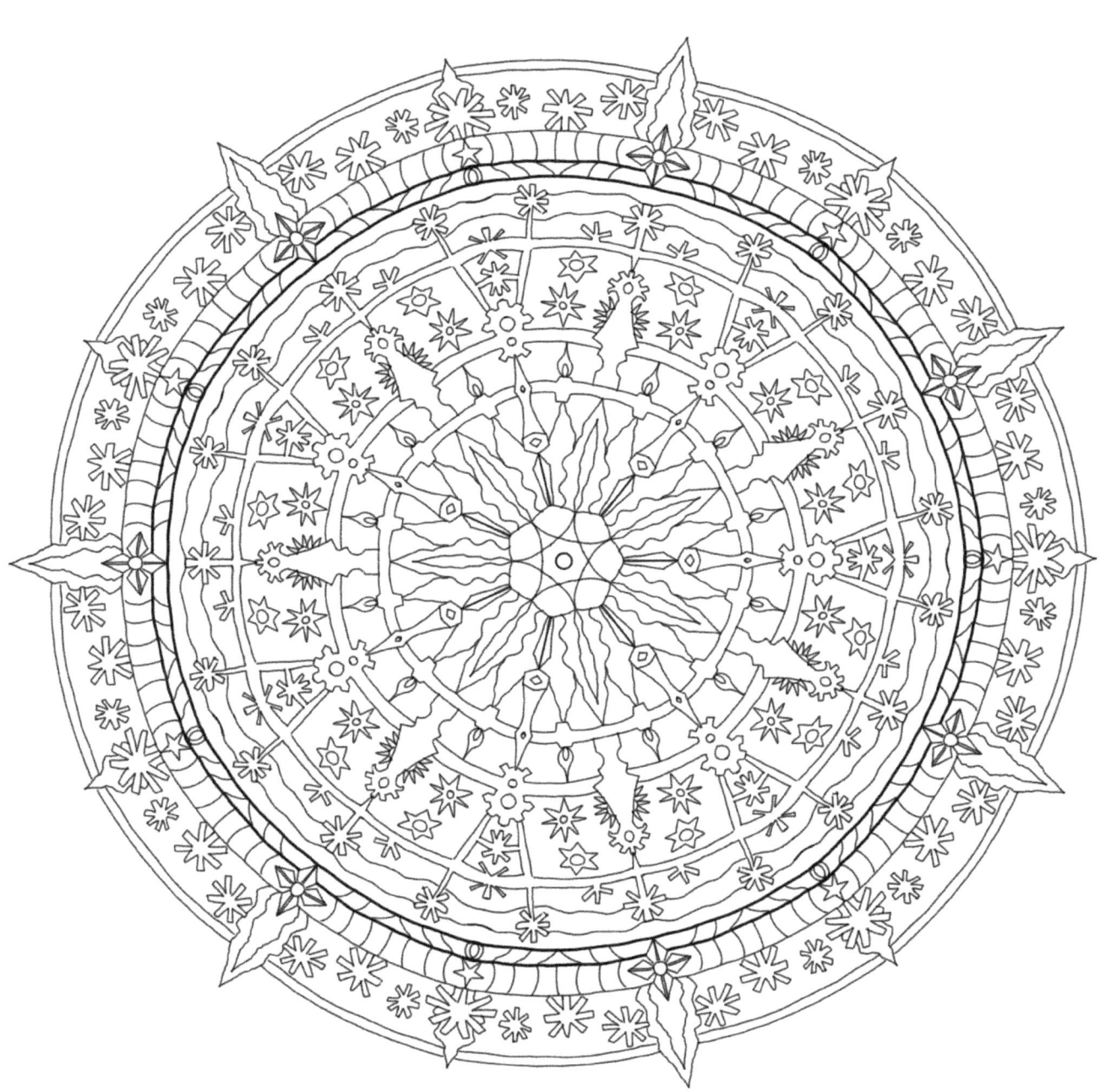

Plate 3

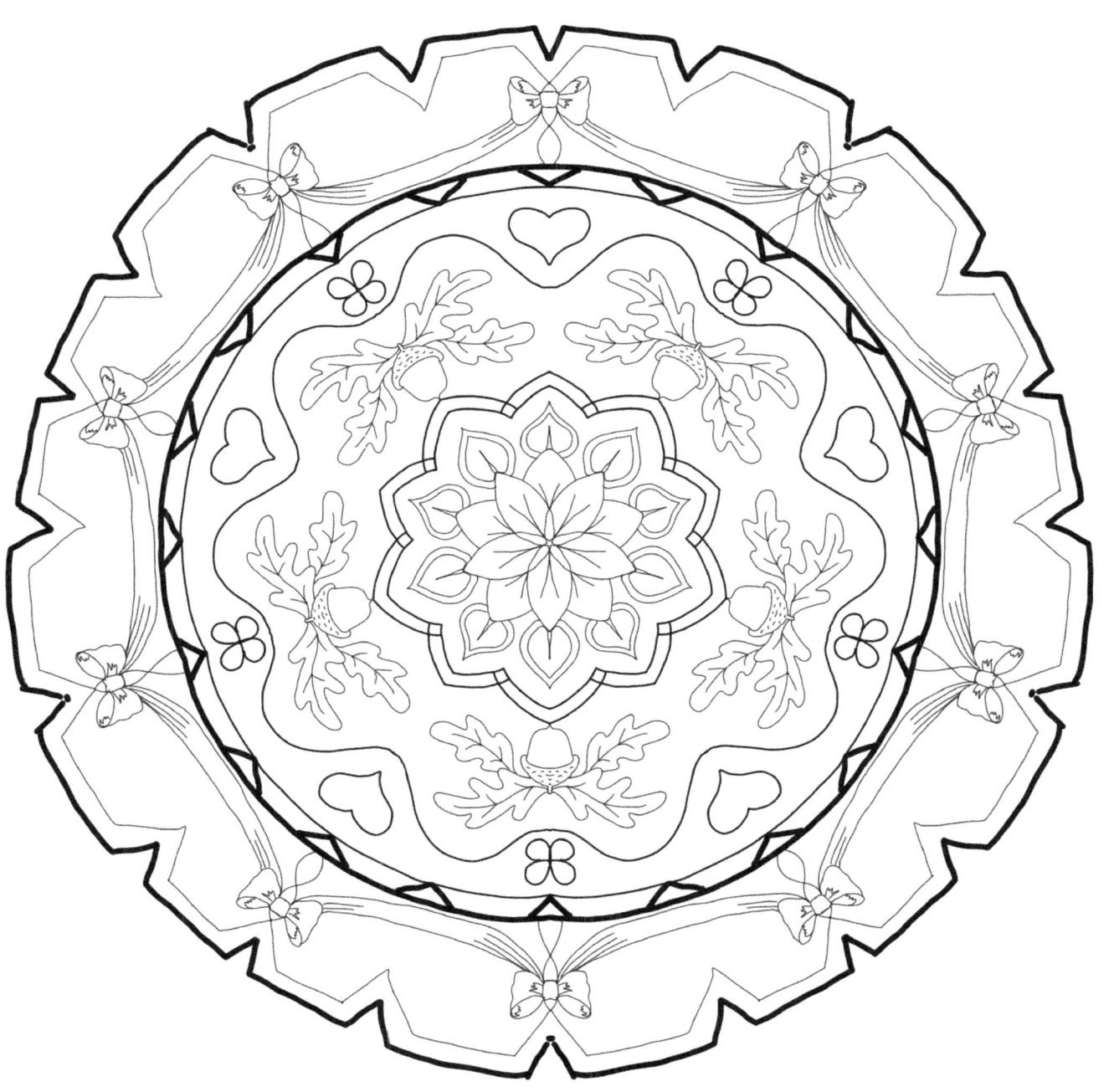

Plate 4

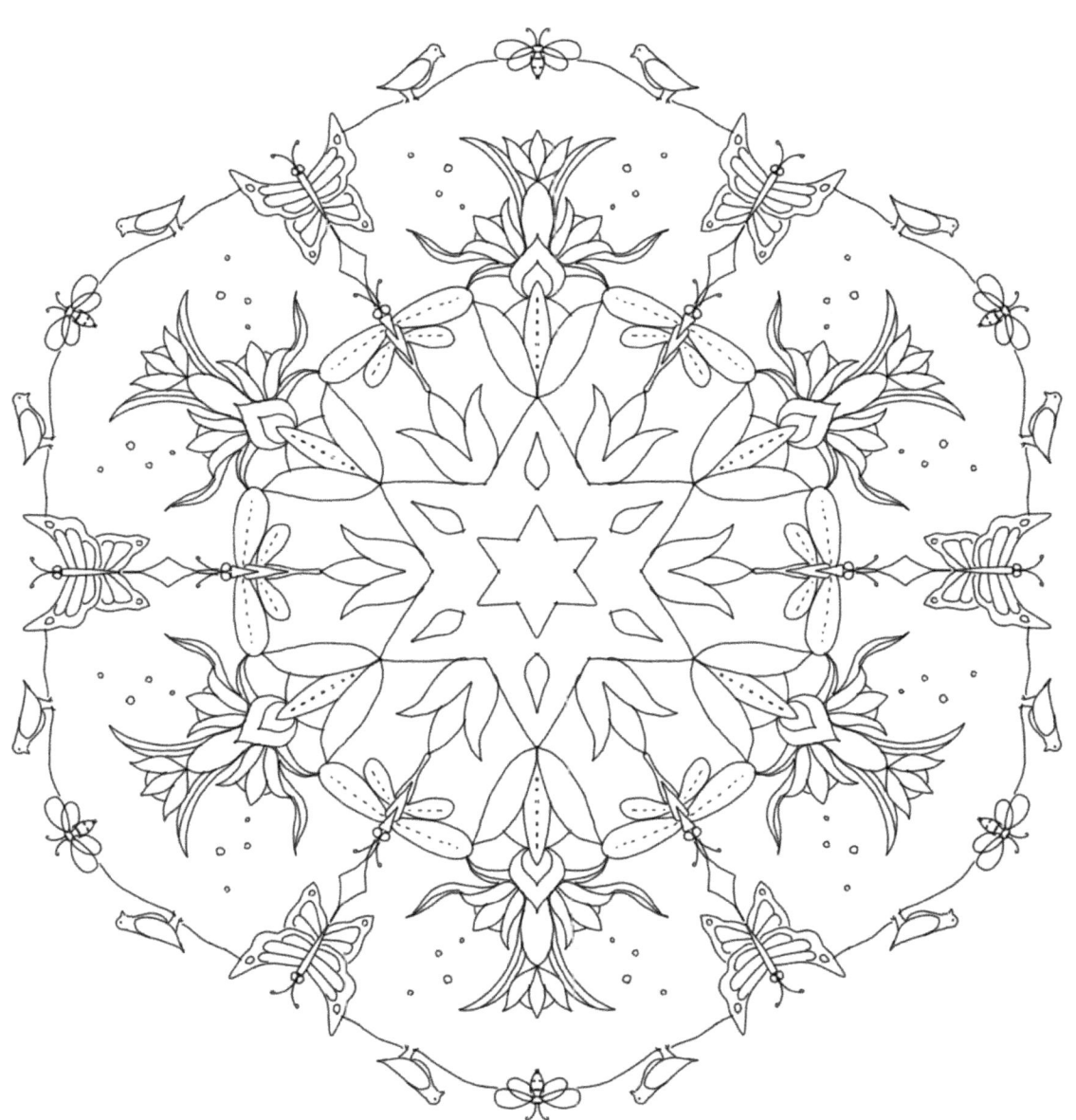

Plate 5

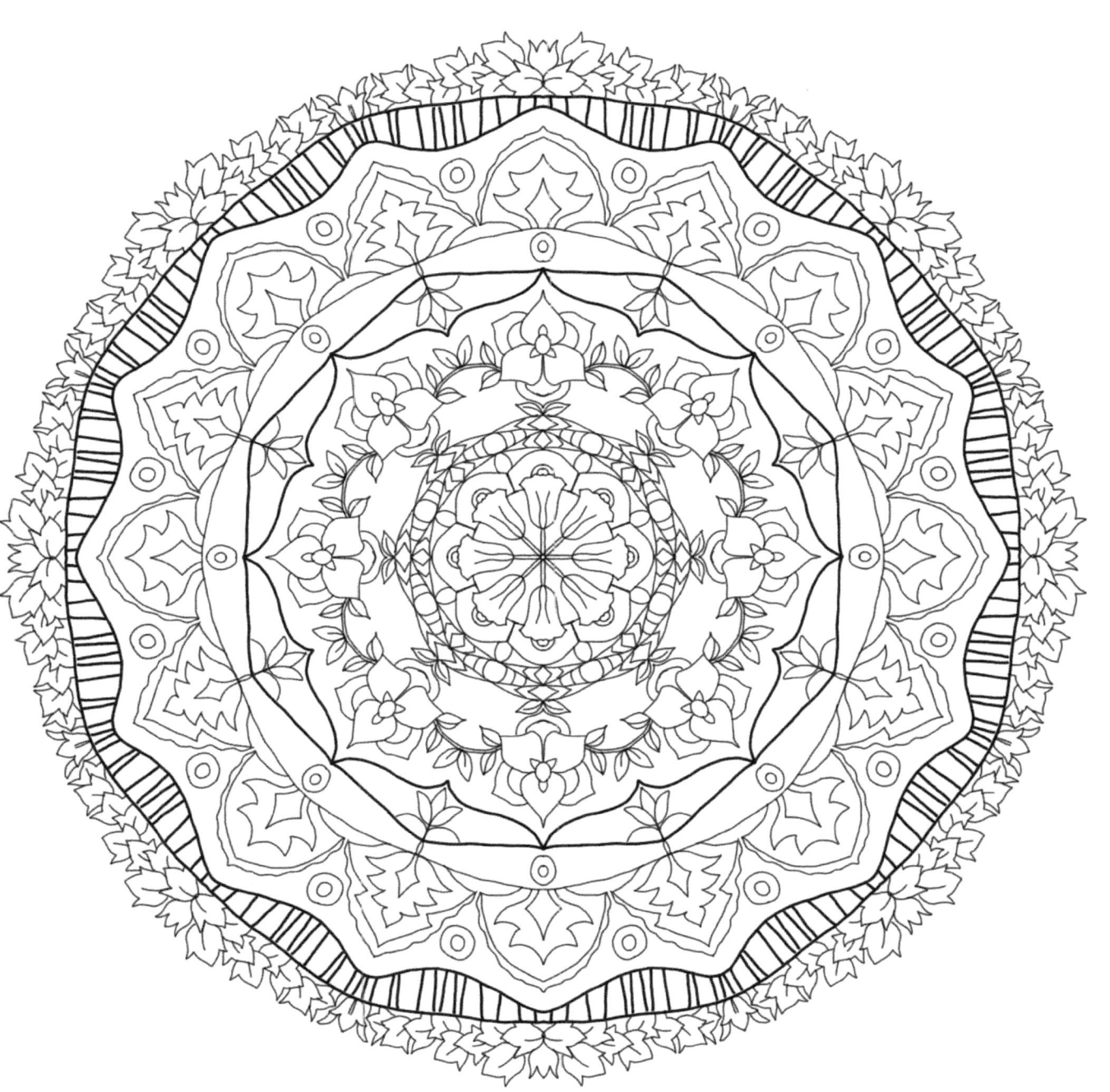

Plate 6

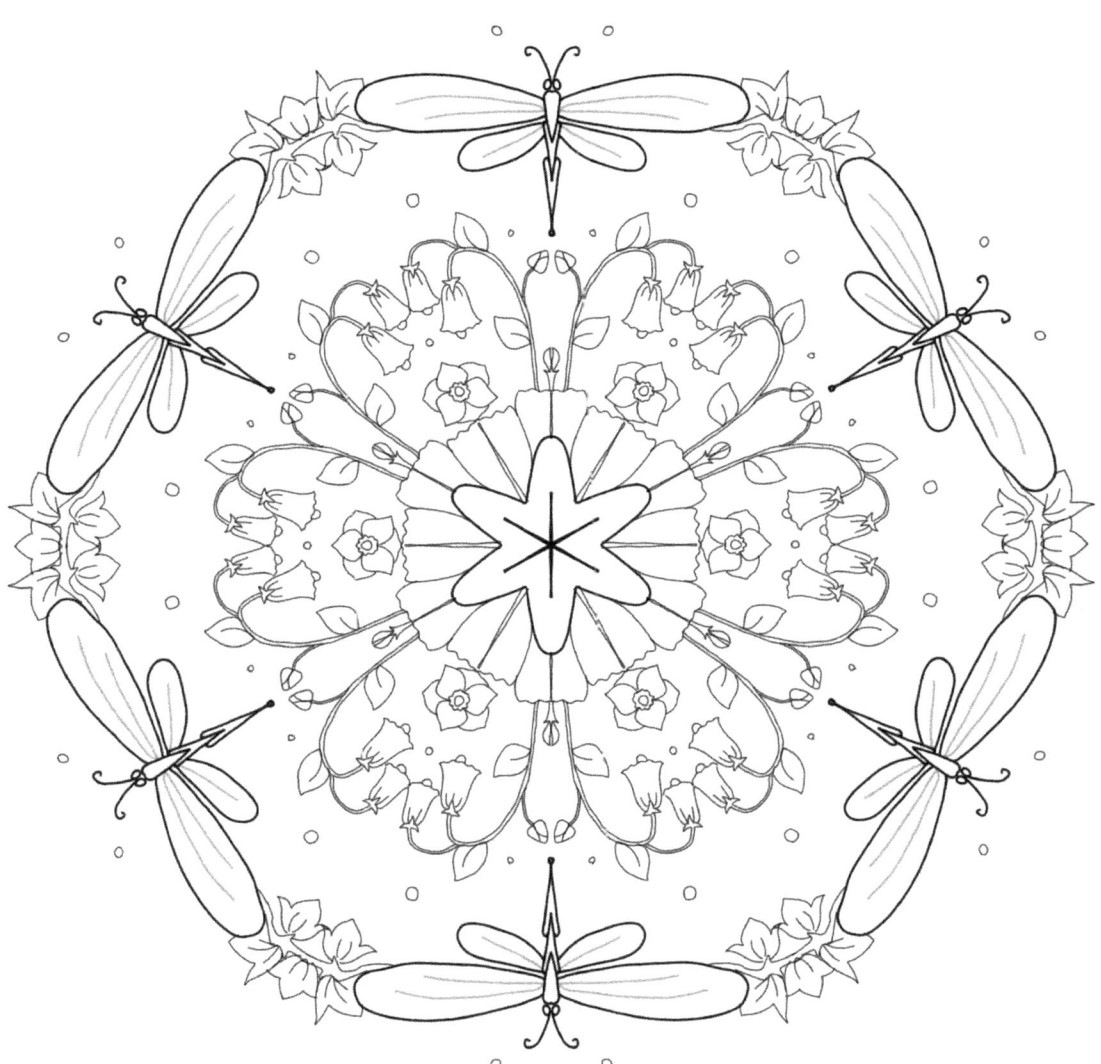

Plate 7

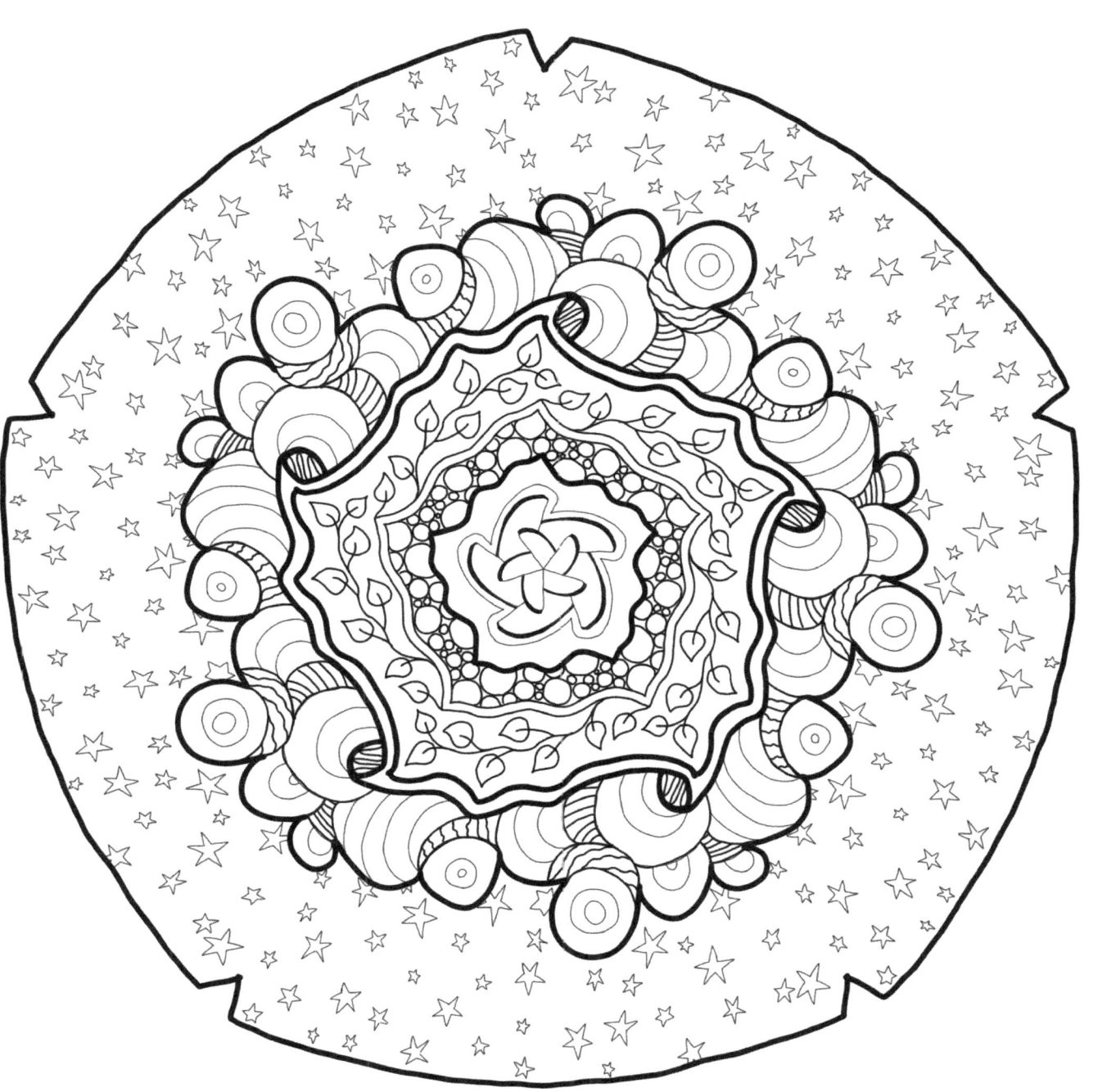

Plate 8

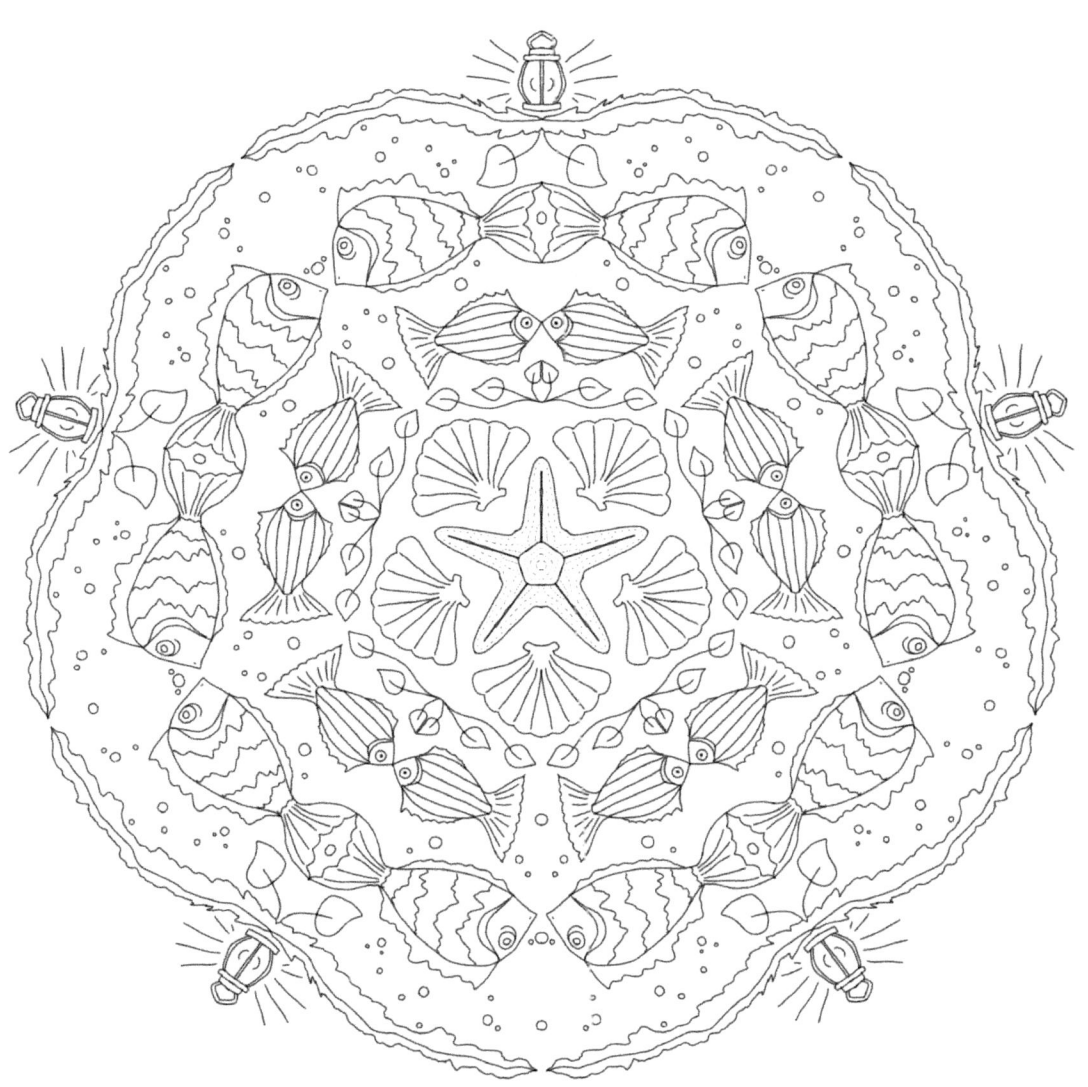

Plate 9

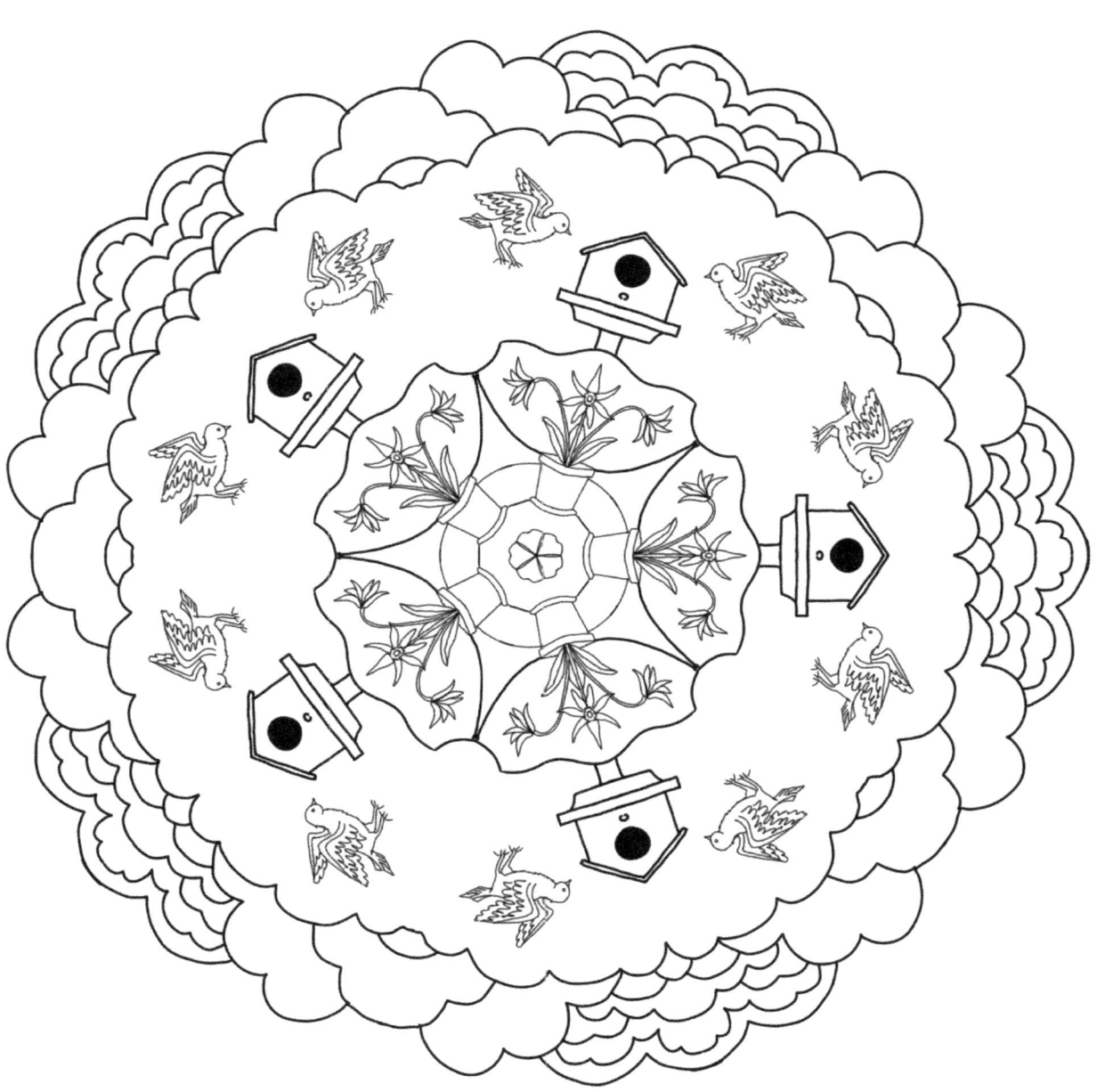

Plate 10

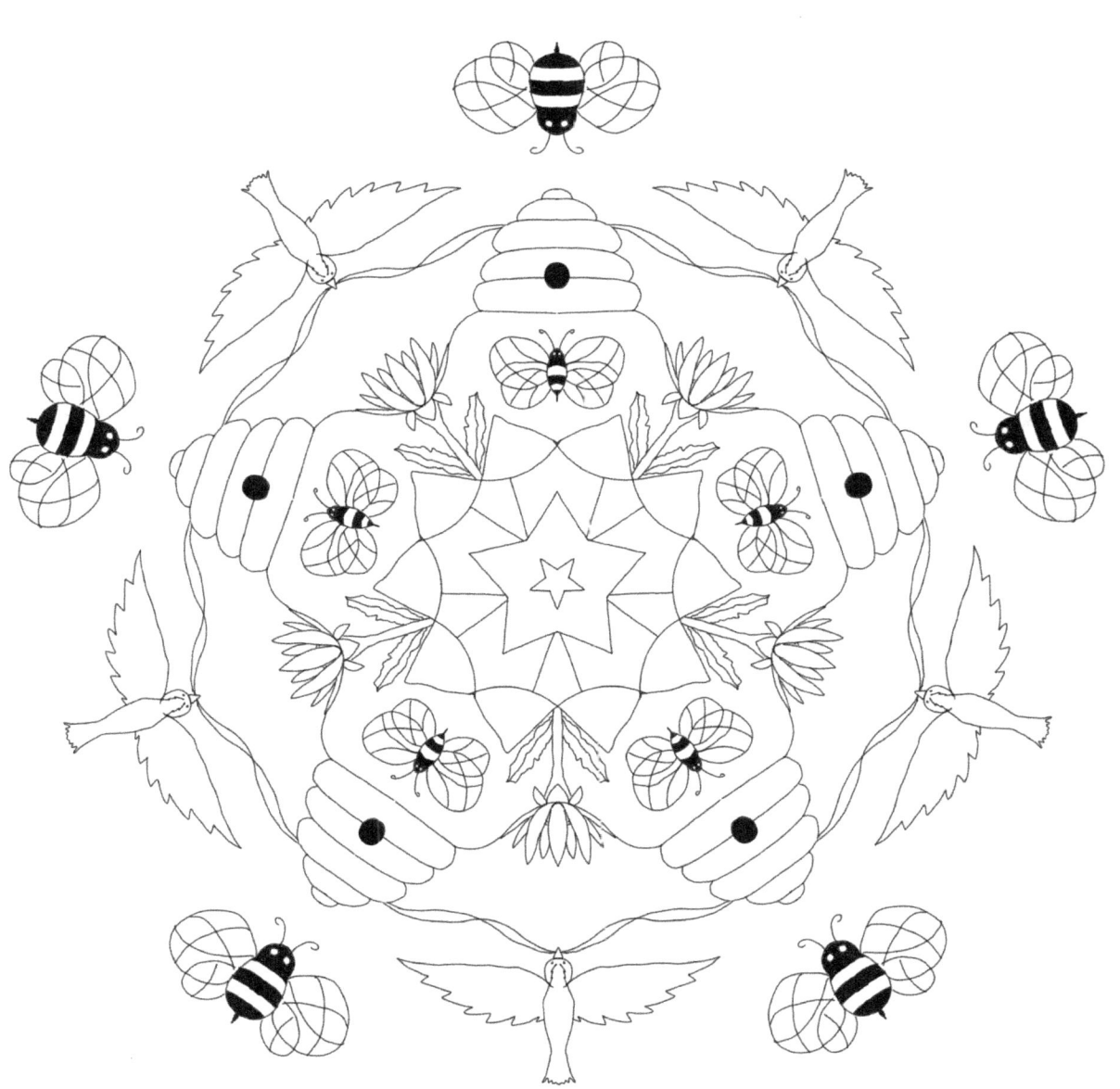

Plate 11

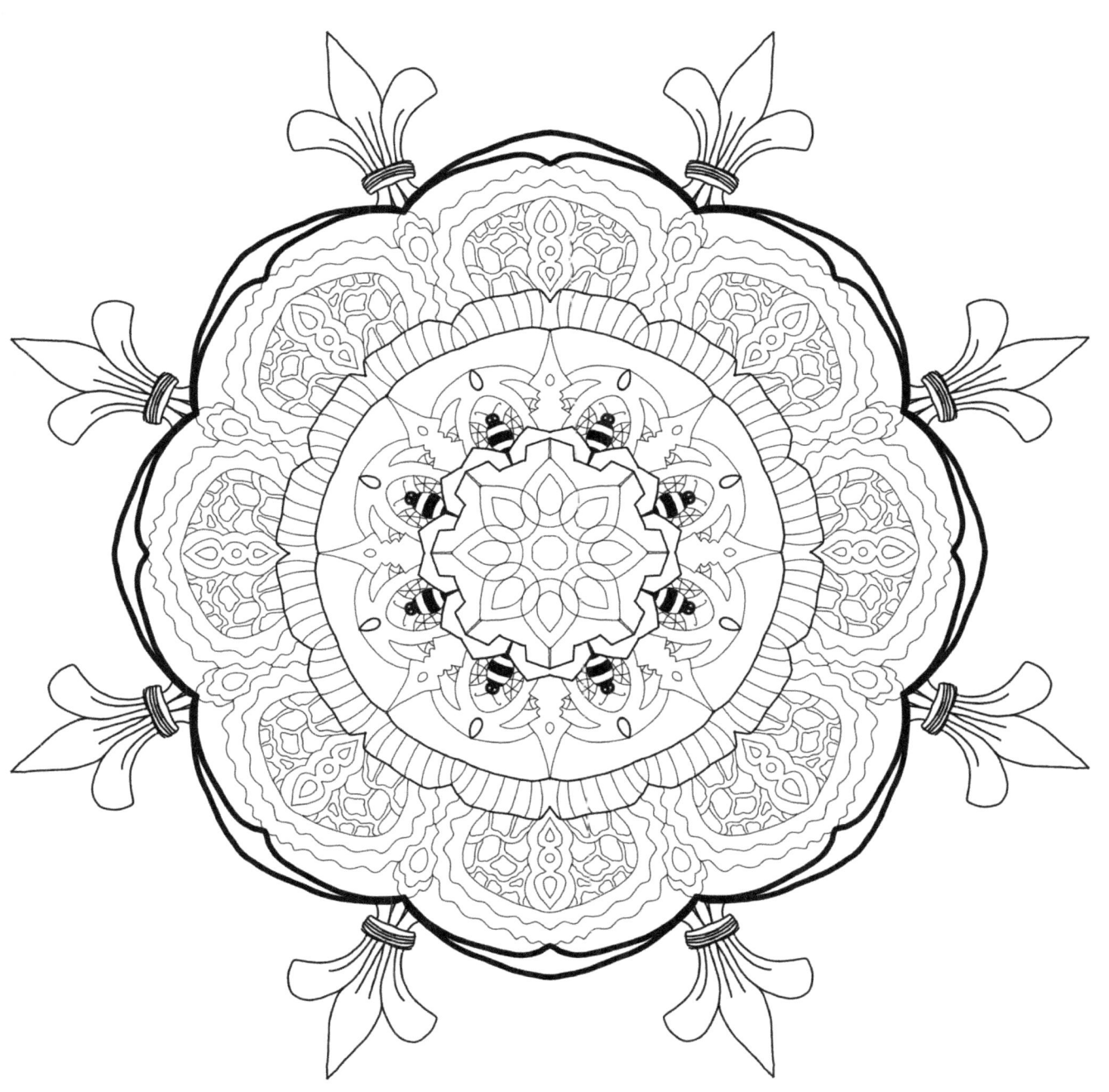

Plate 12

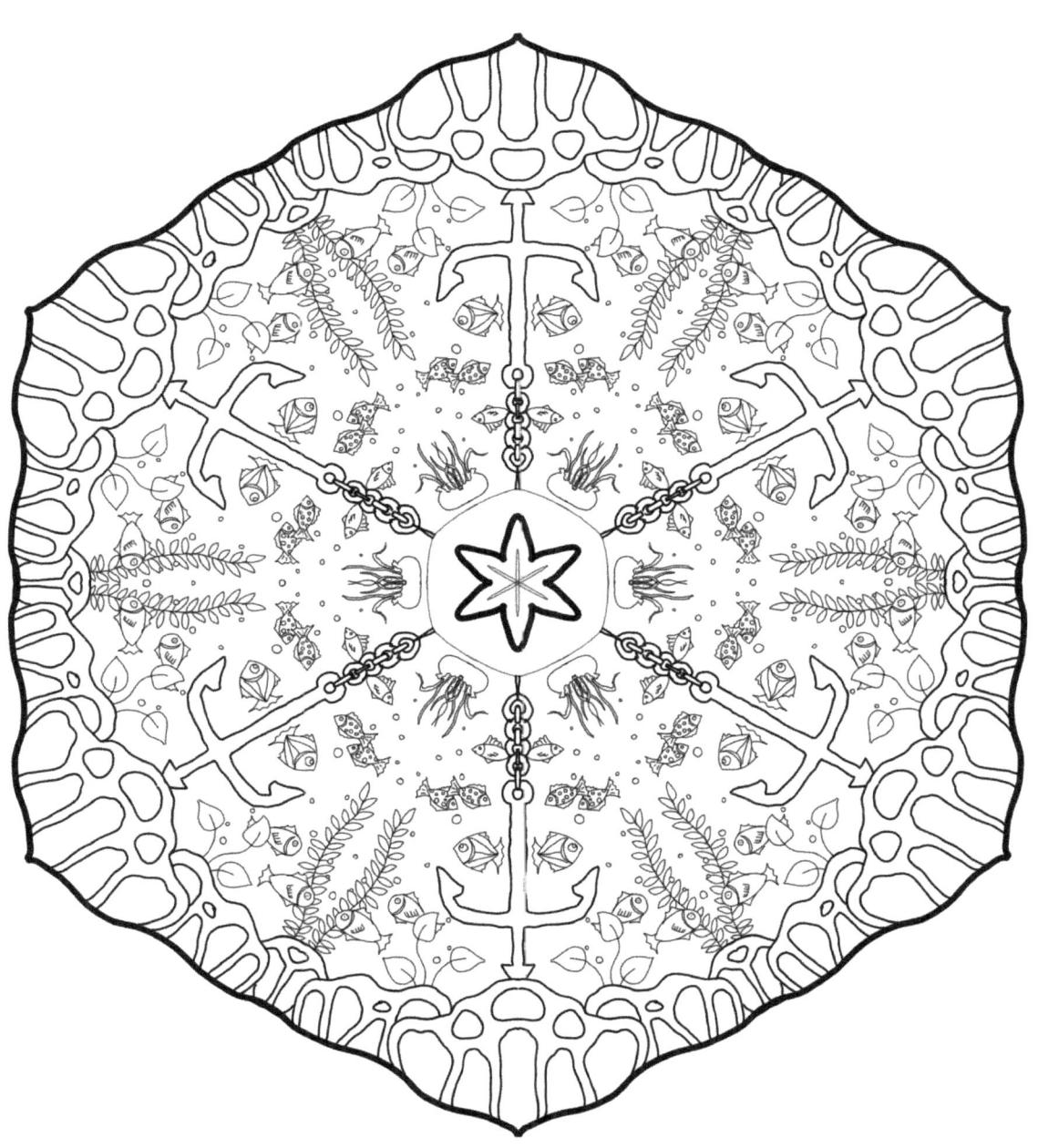

Plate 13

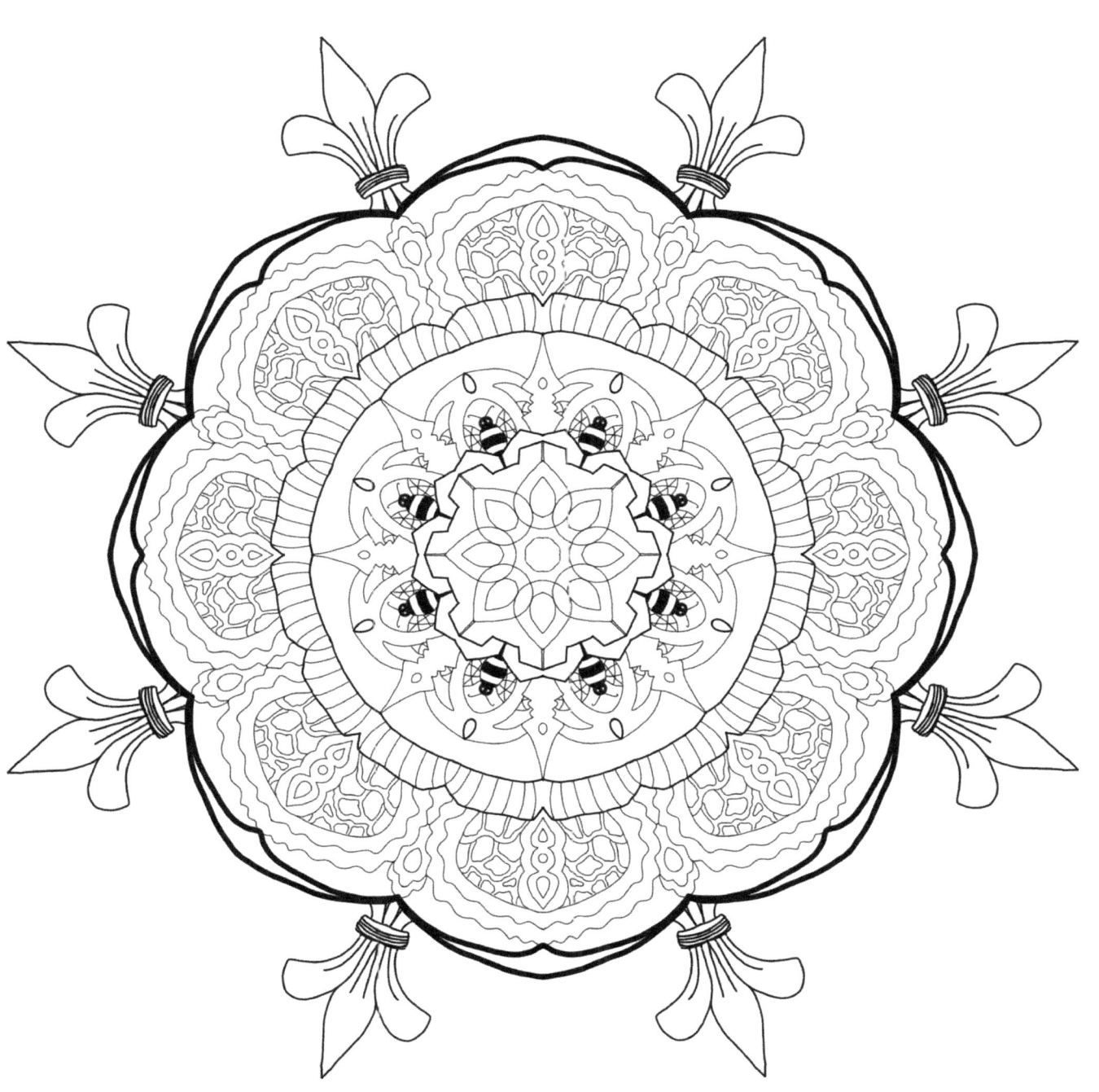

Plate 14

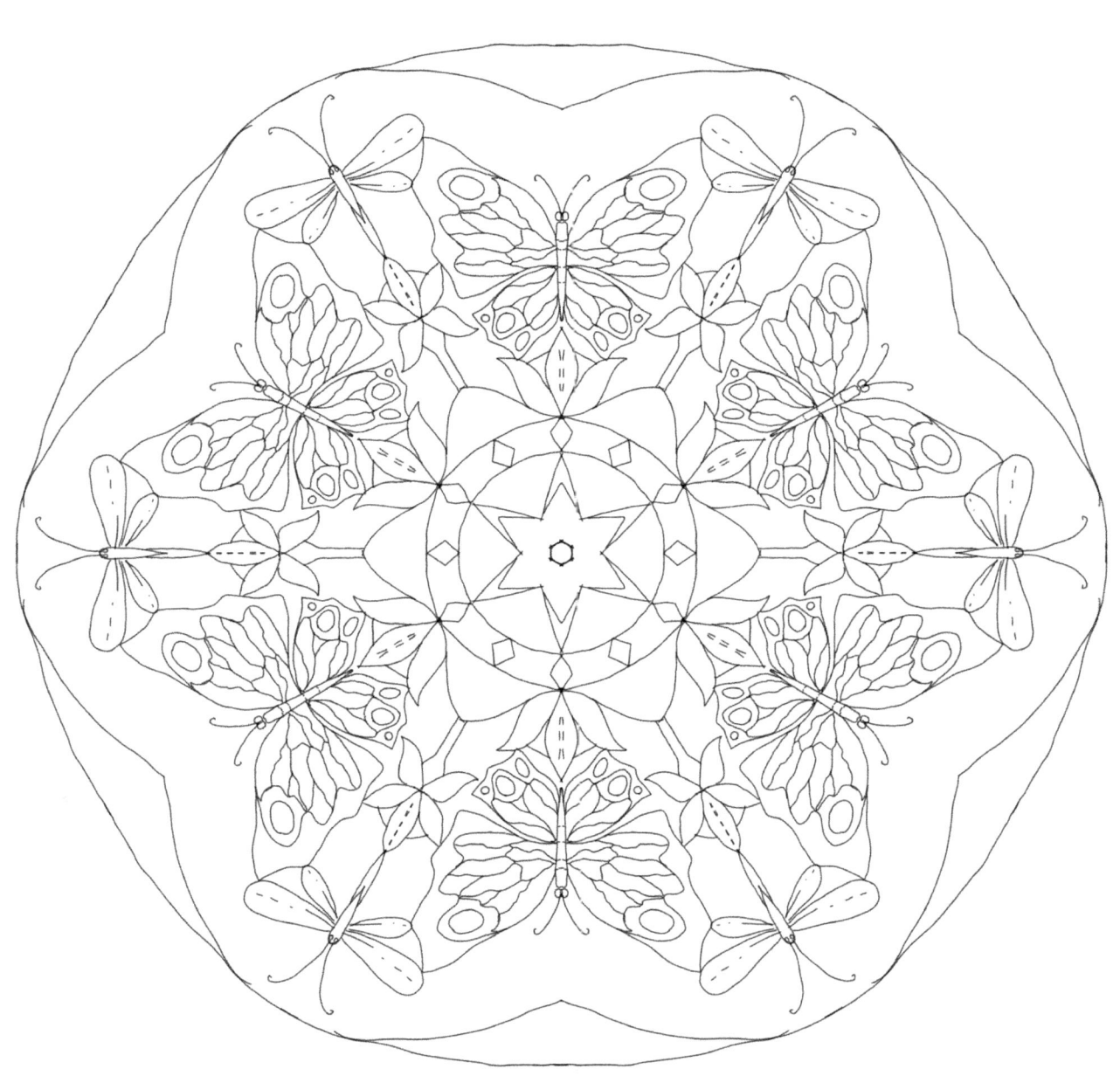

Plate 15

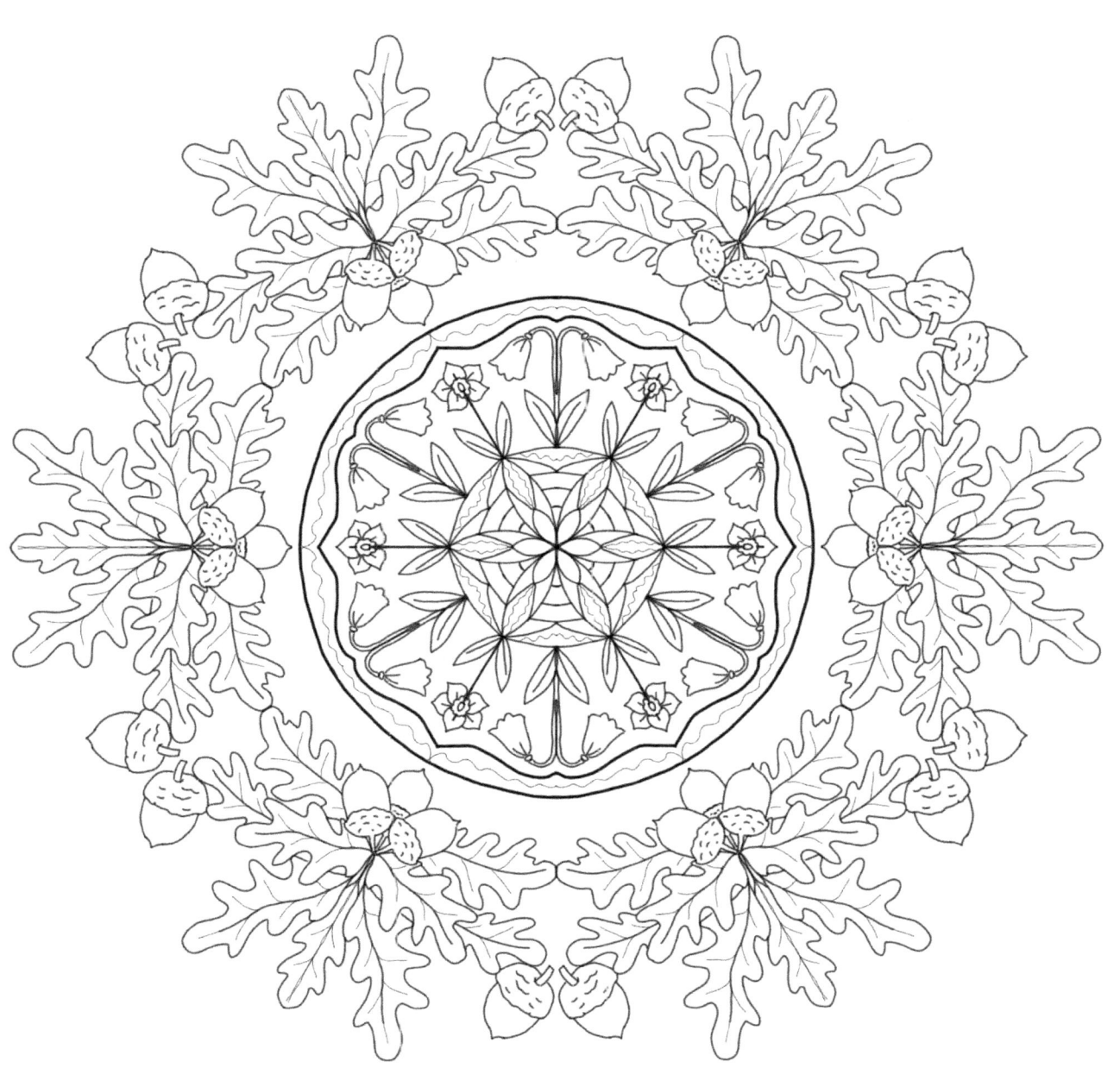

Plate 16

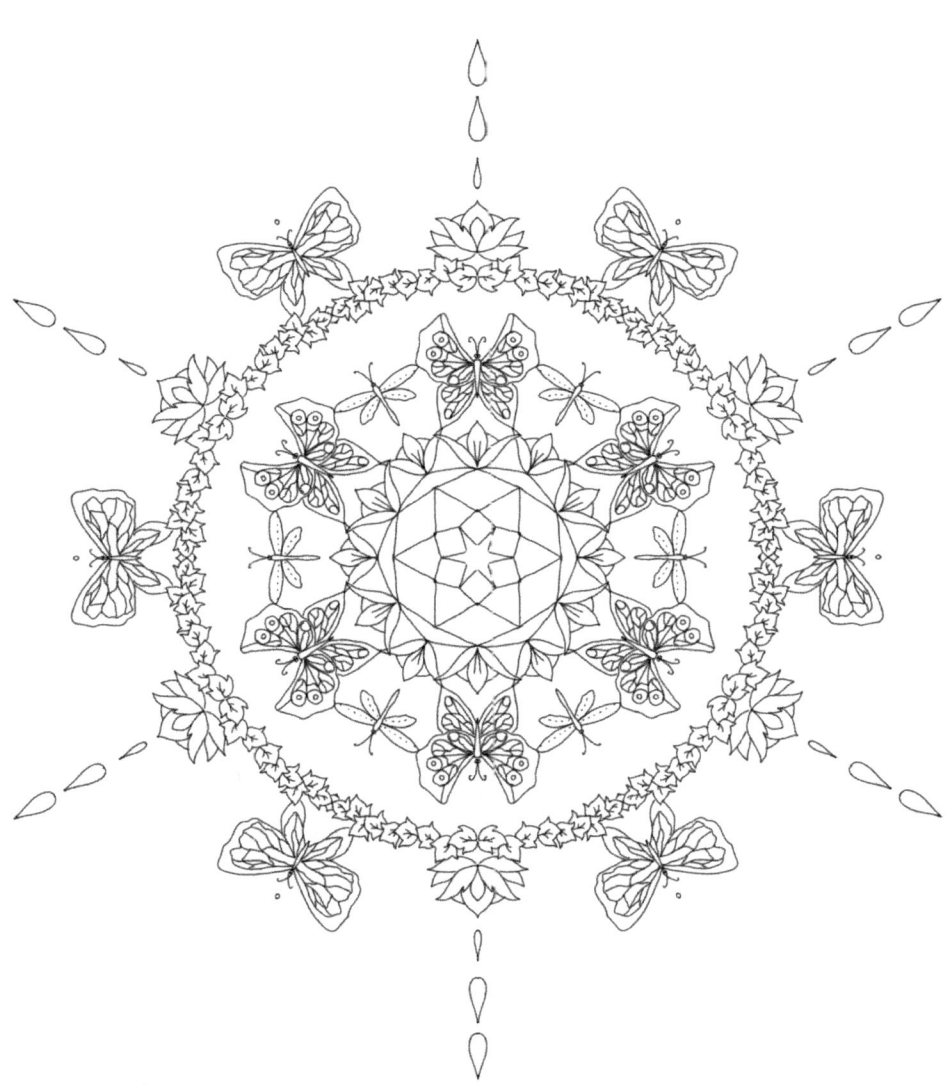

Plate 17

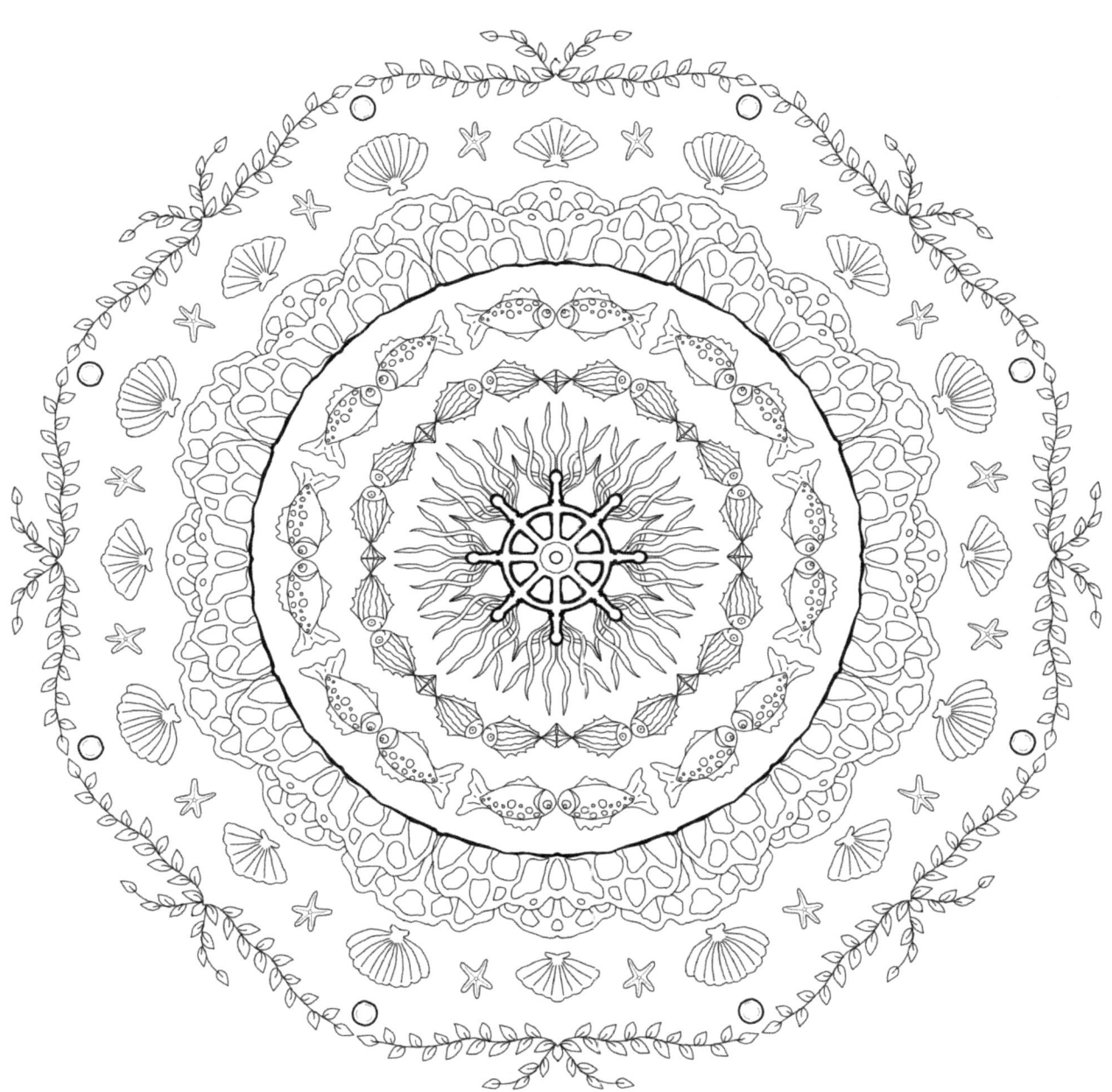

Plate 18

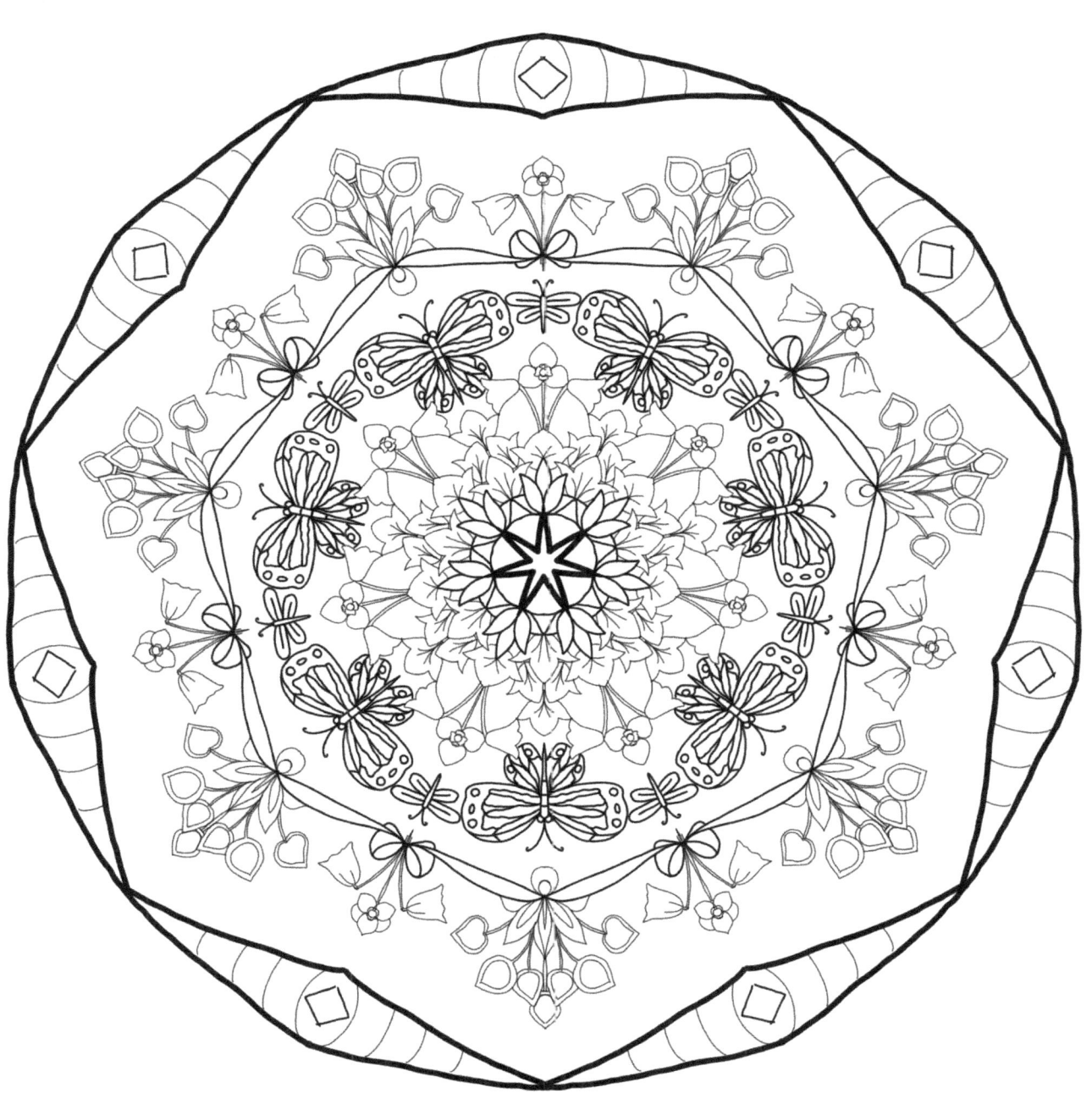

Plate 19

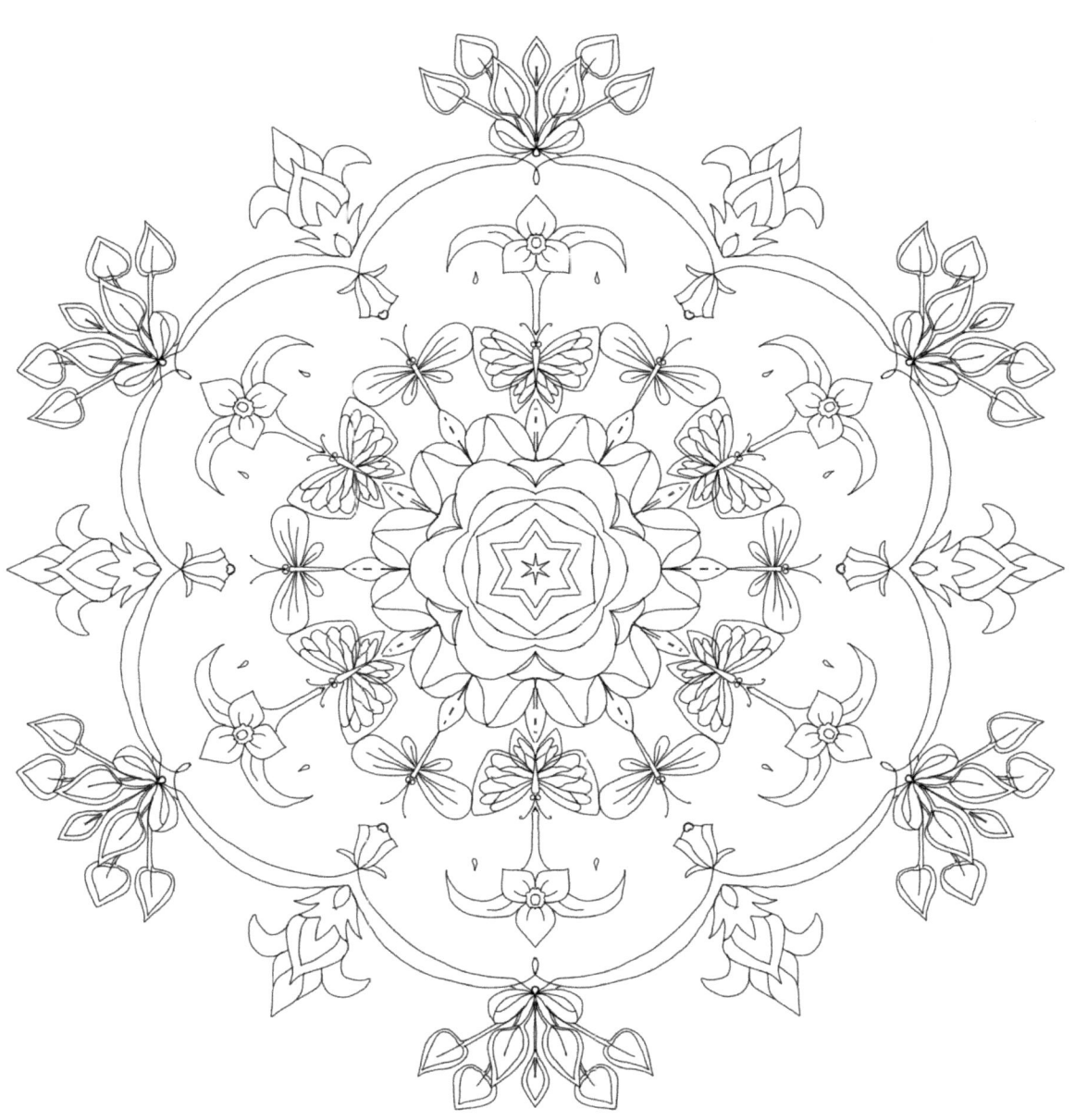

Plate 20

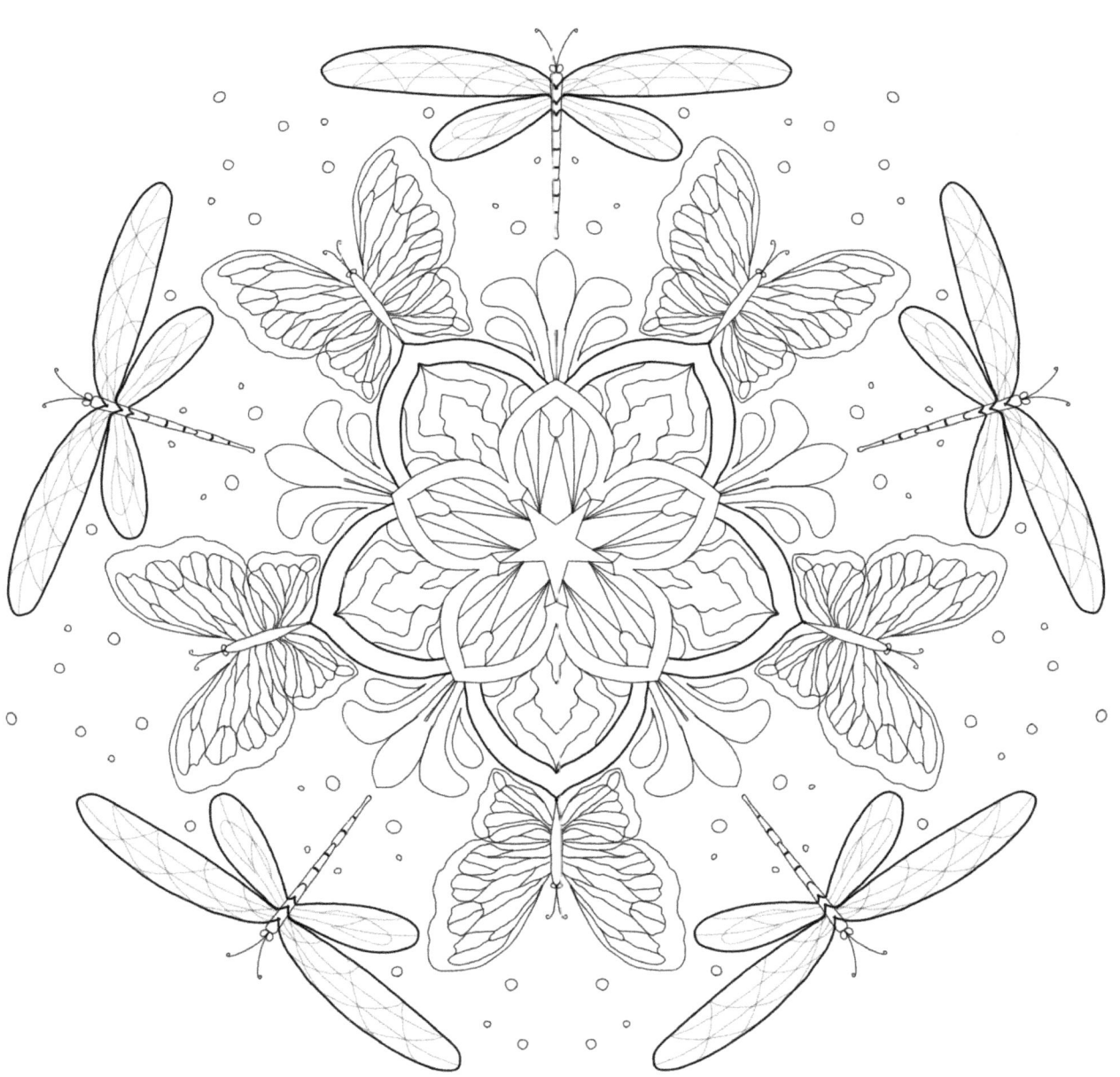

Plate 21

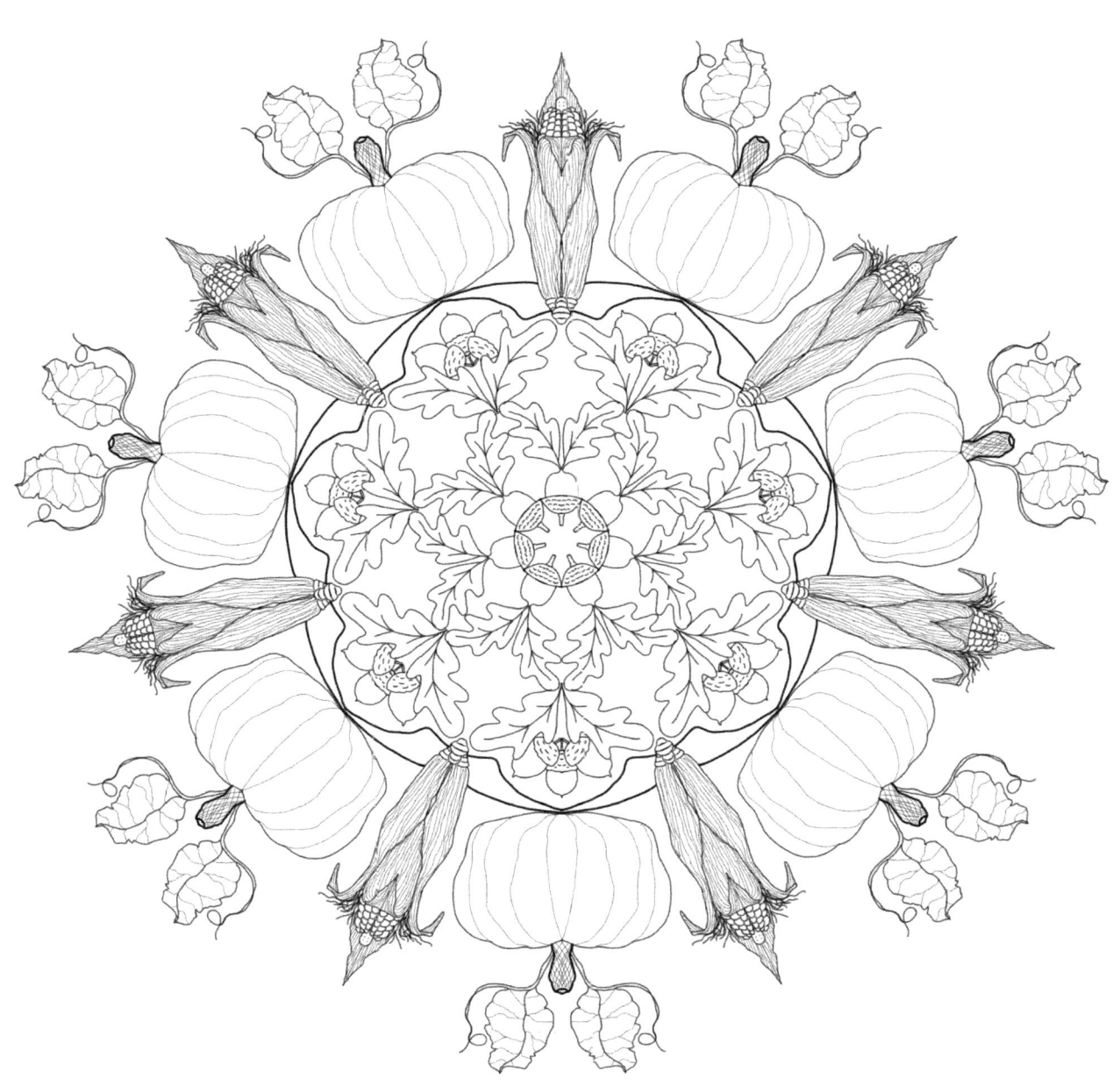

Plate 22

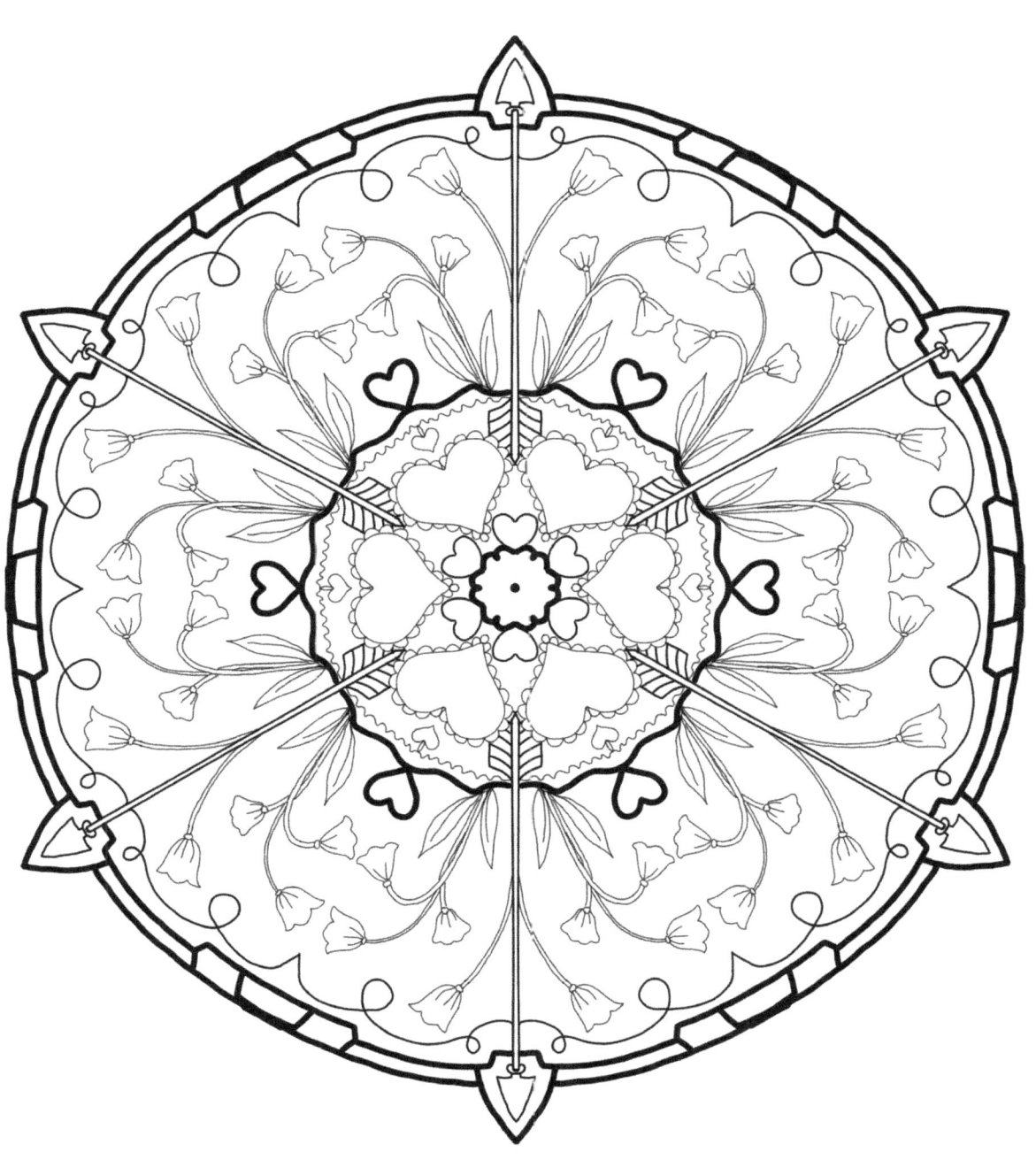

Plate 23

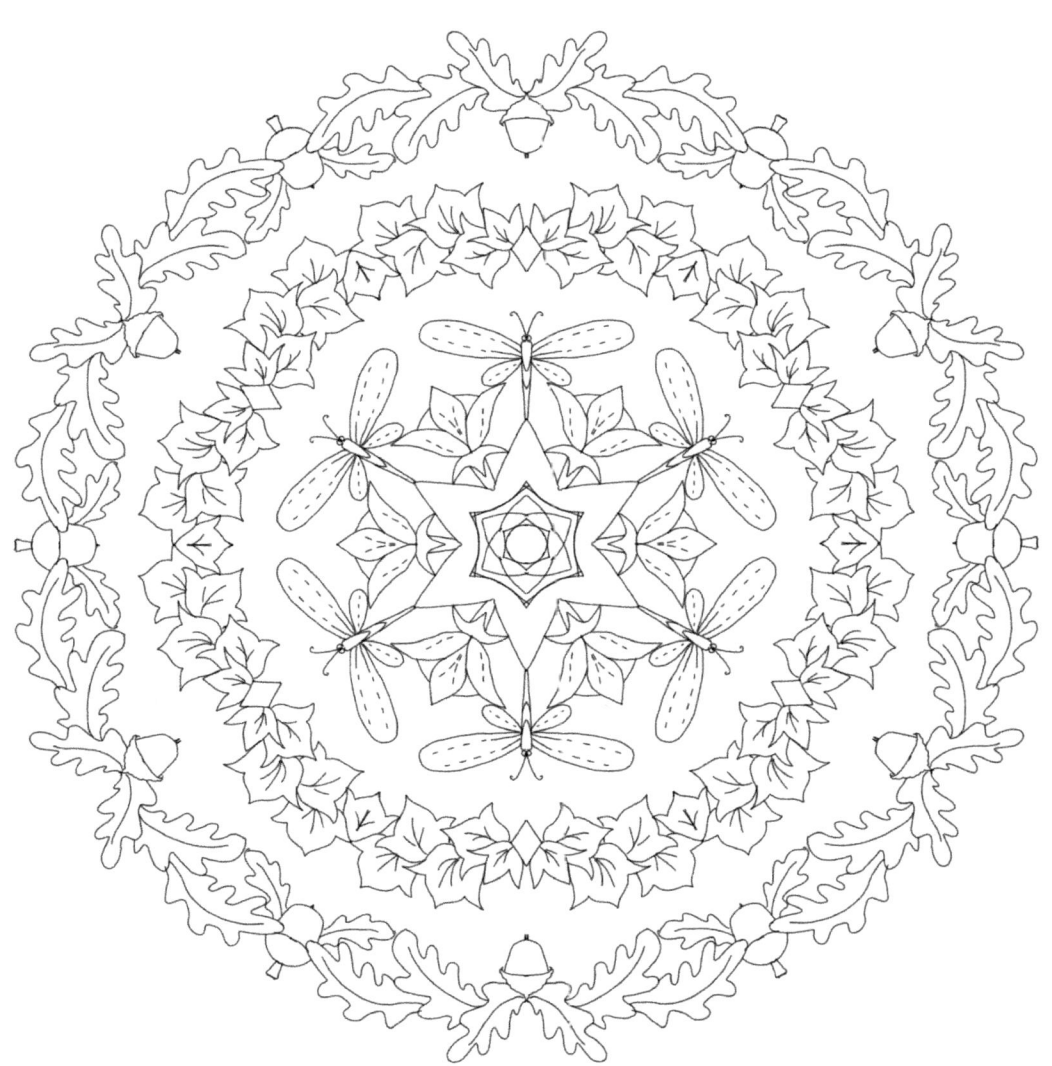

Plate 24

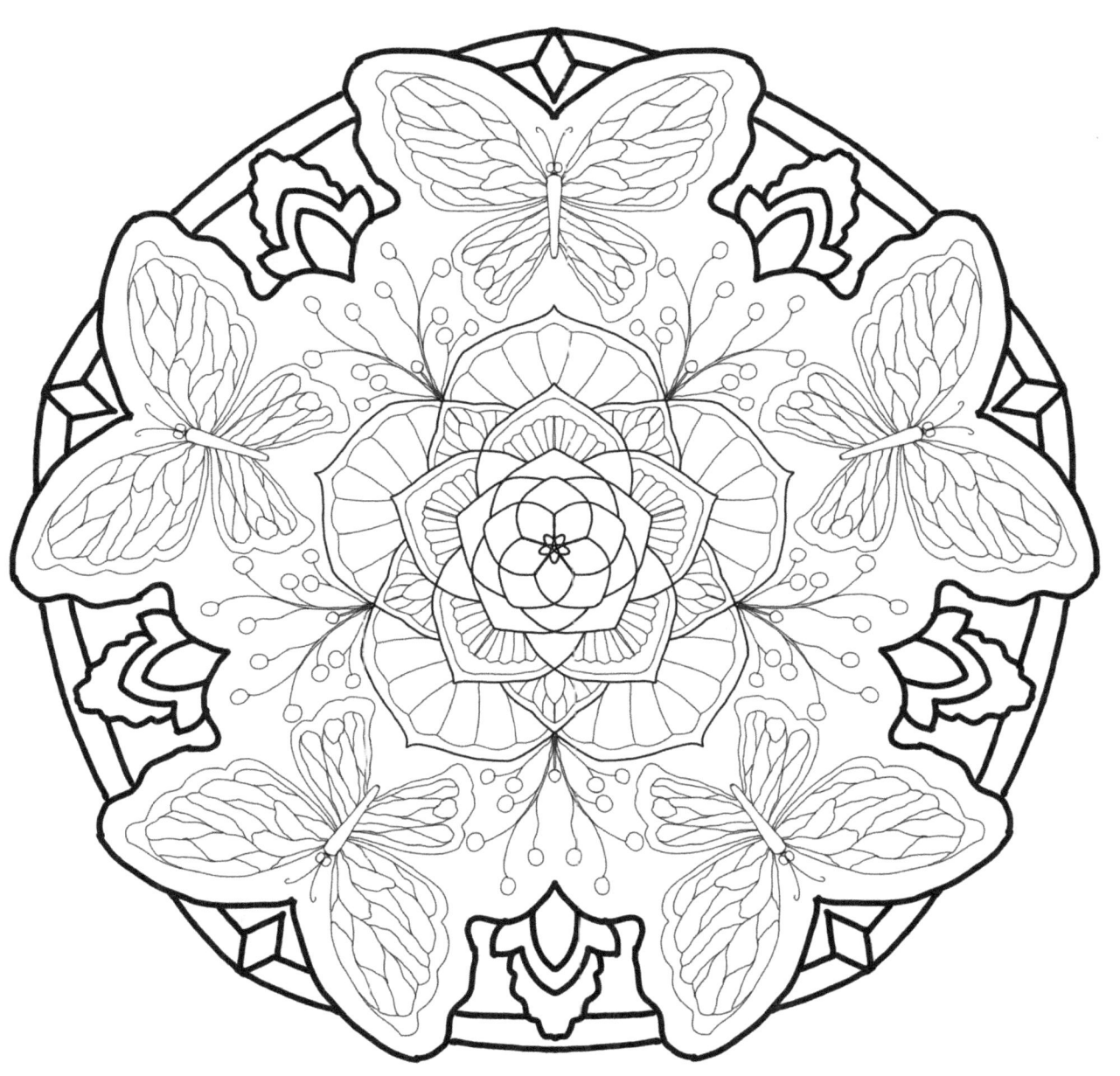

Plate 25

Dear Customer:

I want to thank you for choosing to buy my coloring book. Your decision to buy my drawings is important to me.

Creating and coloring mandalas is an ancient meditative practice. I hope you will find yourself immersed in a creative process as you color which you find beneficial.

Relax, Enjoy and be Creative.

Thank you,
Stacy-Sue Cobb

www.ingramcontent.com/pod-product-compliance
Lightning Source LLC
Chambersburg PA
CBHW080908220526
45466CB00011BA/3506